GOALS

SECRET TO SETTING AND ACCOMPLISHING

Forward

Hello! First off, I want to tell you how happy it makes me that you are taking this step forward towards improving your life. The reason I created this book isn't for money, fame or some other sort of glory. I wrote this book because this content is missing from the world. A while back I was on the internet looking for a book that I could write down my goals in. In my search I came across journals, notebooks and many different variations of planners. I found everything besides what I was looking for. In my frustration I decided to make my own personal book, where I could write down my goals. As I started creating this book, ideas started to flow. I began to reflect on my past goals and I asked myself, "Did I actually accomplish these?". I took out my previous yearly goals journal and noticed pages of vague goals left in the graveyard of years past. All full of potential, and, all unaccomplished.

After some reflection and thought, I had an "ah ha" moment. I asked myself, "Do I really know how to accomplish a goal? How to create a goal? How to structure a goal? What separates the goals I accomplish from the goals I failed to accomplish?". The answer was obvious. Each accomplished goal followed the same process and structure.

When we think of a goal, we look into the future at an outcome that is very much possible. We literally have a vision. In the new year we see millions of people having visions of themselves getting into shape, making more money, being more positive, etc. They all start with a vision, and eventually they give up, forget, or on the rare side, pull through and accomplish their goal. The reason we give up and forget isn't because we are lazy or unmotivated, it's because we lose consistency and stop at the vision stage. Now the question is - how do we create a vision that is consistent?

With many many years of trial and error in my own personal goals, fitness goals or multi-million dollar business goals, I have developed the SECRET to setting goals and actually completing them. If you are ready to take your life to the next level, you came to the right place. Take your time to read the following information, understand the concepts and, when you're ready, use the following pages to create your own goals in a way that will bring success and positive results.

GOAL SETTING

THE SECRET TO SETTING GOALS AND ACTUALLY COMPLETING THEM

The very first thing we all do when we have a goal we want to attain is envision the expected outcome- also known as our vision. Like we briefly went over in the forward of this book, a vision is a glimpse of future possibilities. We write down a goal to make more money, go to the gym, to eat clean foods and to spend more time with people we love. Every goal we write down has an expected positive outcome. I can bet that no one has ever written a goal down because they sincerely want their life to get worse. It just doesn't make sense to wish things would go negatively in your life. The reason you get inspired by your goals at the beginning of creating them is the simple fact that it brings you into a positive state of mind. You see a version of yourself that is better in some way. That version of you is 100% achievable. Being positive and keeping that positivity in your life will not only help you accomplish your goals but it will have a HUGE impact in all aspects of your life. There is a big secret that is shared throughout the world of success seekers. It's honestly not really a secret, but it's so simple that most people won't do it. That "secret" is to have a positive attitude. Having a positive mindset and attitude will help you with your goals in a ton of ways from being able to bounce back from failures, to making correct decisions when emotions come into play.

With big goals will come big failures. It's just the way it goes, the universe likes to work this way I suppose. The more you want to achieve, and the greater version of yourself you want to become, the more failures and obstacles you will encounter. Steve Harvey, one of the people I really look up to, put it this way - " I have failed far more times than I have succeeded. Far more. You will never succeed more than you fail. That's not how it works. You know why? Because failure is a wonderful teacher. It's the only way to learn. You have to fail. Failure is a part of the process to becoming successful." - Steve Harvey.

You will fail. There is no getting around it- but having that positive outlook on failure as a teacher and a learning lesson rather than a setback will help you continue the path to achieving your goal. It will keep you consistent. One goal that always comes around on New years eve is one of getting into shape. The gyms are packed for about 2-3 weeks then slowly the population diminishes and it gets back to how it usually looks. These people who quit either didn't see results fast enough or failed at keeping their consistent schedule. Instead of bouncing back, they just quit all together and failed to reach their vision. The falling out may be gradual. They may miss one day and keep going, then next week miss 2 days. Eventually they just stop going. They lose interest and sight of the vision they had when creating the goal. Just because you may fail in the journey of accomplishing your goals doesn't mean you have to quit. It means you are learning from your mistakes and have the option to get back to your journey towards a better version of yourself.

When we start the process of setting goals we get these ideas and thoughts in our heads and build up enough courage to write them down. The process of writing down your goal is a mental contract with yourself. This is about as far as most of us get. We just write down goals and get to it. The part that's missing is your signature. In any contract, your signature is a symbol that says you will follow all the terms and conditions within the contract. You can back out of any contract without your signature, but once the signature is applied you're now obligated to fulfill the contract. Your signature is equivalent to finding out your WHY.

Why do you want your goal to be accomplished? Why should you work so hard, why is your goal so important? Identifying this foundation for every goal will make them more meaningful, as you now have a connection to the goal. Let's say your goal is to go to the gym. Ask yourself why. Why do you want to go to the gym? Is it because you want to live a healthier lifestyle, or want a better body type to feel more comfortable going to the beach? Whatever it is, dig deep. Figure out the reason you want to set the goal and use this as a reminder of why you're going to the gym. Let's say you never set your why and you're just going to the gym because it's a goal and you want to look stronger. This may motivate you for a little while but compare this to a goal that has a deep meaning. You want to go to the gym because you are a little self conscious about your image and packing on some more muscle or less fat will make you feel more comfortable and give you confidence. You want to be healthier so you can live a longer more fulfilling life. This why is powerful and has meaning so you will most likely stick to the goal a little longer. There's a few methods you can use to structure your goal to help you achieve it at an even greater level.

Ok, so to start with, let's review the basics of goal setting. In order to do this we are going to review S.M.A.R.T goals created in 1981 by George Doran, Arthur Miller, and James Cunningham. This is a technique used by many professionals in order to make sure your goals are on the right track. It was written for a paper called "There's a S.M.A.R.T way to write management goals and objectives." In the document he introduced the S.M.A.R.T goals method as a way to improve the chances of a goal to succeed and be accomplished. The 5 letters in S.M.A.R.T are an acronym that means the following.

S.   Specific. Your goal should be clear and specific. Rather than saying I want to lose weight as compared to stating you want to fit into a specific set of jeans. This helps you focus your efforts and feel truly motivated. An easy way to make a specific goal is to apply the commonly asked questions - the 4 **W**'s. **W**hat do I want to accomplish? **W**hy is this goal so important? **W**ho is involved? **W**here is this taking place?

M.   Measurable. Having goals that are measurable is crucial because it allows you to track your progress and stay motivated. You'll know exactly what needs to be done. Having a way to measure progress helps you stay focused, meet deadlines, and feel the excitement and motivation to keep going by moving closer to achieving your goal. For example, you might say that you want to lose a certain amount of weight by a certain date. This allows you to track and measure your progress. An easy way to make sure your goal is measurable is by using the commonly asked questions - 3 **H**'s. **H**ow many? **H**ow much? **H**ow will I know when it is accomplished?

A. Achievable. It's important to dream big but make sure it's actually attainable. For example - I love Soccer (Futbol) I am not super tall, I'm kind of athletic, in pretty good shape, I know my limits though. I know I can't go and be a soccer star playing for PSG, but I CAN share leadership and mindset skills to some of the players and personally get to know the team... In other words, dream big but know your limits. Your goals should stretch your abilities but still remain possible. As you set goals most of them will be 100% possible, the only limit is your mindset. Ask yourself the following questions. How realistic is the goal based on your constraints? What can you do to make this an achievable goal? 9/10 times you CAN accomplish your vision, the other 1/10 is a vision that may have to be re-adjusted because of constraints.

R. Relevant. This is to make sure your goals matter to you and are aligned with your other goals. The particular goal you are working on, during and when achieved, should push your other goals forward. Think of working on one of the following F's: Family, Faith, Freedom, Finances, Fun, Friends, and Fitness. If your goal is to have a nice lifted truck and a couple UTV's, this is in alignment with - Fun, Family, Freedom, Finances, etc. You need money to get this, so you need to focus on working on finances, once you get it you can enjoy spending time with your family while having fun. To get some time off you need to have enough freedom to do so. These all are in alignment with your initial goal. If you just want a nice truck to flex on people, and because someone else has one...That's fine, but it wont drive you as much as a goal that's relevant and has a purpose. A relevant goal can answer "yes" to the following questions - Does this goal seem worthwhile? Does this match/align with your other goals? Am I the right person to reach this goal?

T.   Time-Bound. Every goal needs a target date. If you have a target date you have a deadline that will be CRUCIAL to the following half of the goal setting. Having a target date can also help you keep track of your progress. If you have a goal, for example, of making 1 million dollars. That's good! It's achievable and realistic. Now add a time limit to it. When do you want to make a million by? A year? 5 years? Think about it and set a date.

Once you have mastered the S.M.A.R.T goal now it's time for the part that actually will help you achieve and accomplish your goals. Let's go through the S.M.A.R.T process together. I will provide two examples, one that is more suitable to daily life, and one geared towards a business mindset.

Example 1:

For this goal, let us begin with a general goal of losing weight. We envision ourselves as a beautiful and lean Goddess/God. How can we turn this general goal into a SMART goal?

First we must take our general goal and narrow it down into a Specific goal: I want to lose 20 pounds.

M: Measurable- I know that I need to do this in a healthy way, so i want to lose one pound per week. By pinpointing how much weight I want to lose per week, this allows me to measure how I am progressing towards my goal.

A: Attainable- I know that I have the 20 pounds to lose, and I also know that I have the ability and equipment needed. I have no other health conditions that would make losing 20 pounds too difficult, or unattainable.

Relevant: This is a goal that is important to me as I want to feel confident in myself, and I want to give my dogs a better life by being able to take them on long walks without dying (fun, family). This will also help me by helping me save money on buying bigger clothes (finances).

T: Time- I will accomplish this goal in 5 months, whatever that date may be. I will circle it on the calendar and use it as a deadline to motivate me to complete my goal.

We used weight loss as this is a common goal that many individuals struggle with and eventually fall short on. However, this format can be used for many other things, such as learning a new language, budgeting and saving, academics, and much more!

Example 2:

Let's set a goal of making more money. We can envision our life being less stressful because we aren't worried about bills. Let's get more into detail with this goal

S. Specific. I want to make 100,000 a year by selling a product I have through an online business, it will be just me with no outside help. The business is located in our home and the resources needed are very limited. The product we sell makes $10 profit after all expenses are paid.

M - Measurable. In order to make the money we need to sell a total of 10,000 products at $10 to make $100,000 by the end of the year. We need to increase marketing and sales to reach this goal.

A - Achievable. This goal is achievable because I know my product can sell well enough to reach the 100k goal. I already have some sales and can increase them by marketing and increasing sale avenues.

R - Relevant. This is relevant because my current job isn't cutting it. I want to live a certain lifestyle that I can't live with my current income. Having my own business will allow me to have more free time that I can use to spend time with family and friends.

T - Time bound. I want to achieve this goal in 1 year. I will keep track of monthly sales and adjust as needed to stay on track.

These 2 examples hit every step in the S.M.A.R.T goal system. It's pretty straight forward of what's needed to do in order to accomplish our goal. As you read that you probably thought to yourself "10,000 products to sell...that's going to be impossible". It's a big goal for sure, but it's not as much as it seems. When we have a huge goal we tend to focus on the huge accomplishment and not the process on how to achieve it. Let's take a closer look at that 10,000 product in a year goal. The best way to make this goal mentally achievable we have to break it down in a way that seems doable. .

A year has 12 months, so let's divide that 10,000 by 12 to get our monthly goal. Our monthly goal would be 833.333, we can round that up to 834. If we sell 834 products a month we will eventually reach our

10k goal in 1 year. Let's continue breaking down the goal. There are 4 weeks in a month so let's divide the 834 by 4. Our weekly goal is 208.5, we can round up to 209. If we sell 209 products a week we will eventually reach our 10k a year goal. Once again let's break it down. There are 7 days in a week so let's divide the 209 by 7. Our daily goal is 29.8, we can round up to 30. With this little process of breaking down a huge goal we now can focus on 30 a day rather than 10,000 a year. We know that if we reach our daily goal of at least 30 sales a day we will achieve our overall goal of 10,000 a year. This is applicable to every time-bound goal we may have.

Let's go back to the example of wanting to lose a certain amount of weight. Instead of looking at 20 pounds in 5 months we can break this down to 3-4 pounds a month, which seems more doable than 20 as a whole. It's a mental trick that can help you achieve your goals rather than just leave them in the graveyard of possibilities we all have

This way of breaking down a big goal also allows you to be able to find your daily tasks. There are many times when we give up on a goal because we don't know where to start. We get lost in the idea and outcome of the goal and we lose focus on the process it takes to reach the end. It's like climbing a mountain. We can look at the top all we want but we will never get there until we take the first step. Reverse engineering our goal will give us a fail-proof plan on how to reach the top. Like the example we gave above, we broke down the goal of losing 20 pounds in 5 months into 3-4 pounds a month, as long as we focus on the 3-4 pounds we will reach the end goal of 20. This is a really simple way to make sure you don't get intimidated by your goal and makes sure you have a place to start. We can take this a step further by adding tasks to the breakdown.

Adding tasks to the breakdown will streamline your progress and leave no room for doubting or laziness. In order to lose the 3-4 pounds a week we will have to figure out what our daily plans are to reach that mini goal.

We will have to adjust our diet and exercise schedule to keep consistency. Monday, Wednesday and Fridays will be leg days and Tuesday, Thursday, Saturday will be upper body days. We will create a weekly diet plan that will keep us on track. With adding these simple tasks we will know exactly what we have to do every day and finishing the day right means we are 100% on track to achieving our 5 month overall goal.

Now that we have shown you how to create goals and structure them in a way that attracts success, we've included some blank pages for you to write down some personal goals you want to complete.

Remember, we can teach you all you want and you can read 1,000 books on how to create a goal, but without action a goal is just a dream. Take action now and make your dreams a reality!

____

____

____

____

____

____

____

____

____

____

____

____

Congratulations! You successfully set some goals!

OR, you just scanned through this workbook and noticed some random text... either way, I just wanted to add some motivation at the halfway mark of this workbook.

As you set goals make sure you don't limit yourself. You are capable of amazing things. If you were to travel back 100 years and tell someone that in the future there will be huge pieces of metal capable for flying through the air hundreds of miles an hour while carrying hundreds of people, you would be called a witch and be burned alive. Luckily, we are less extreme now and you will just get made fun of for having huge unrealistic goals. Look at Elon Musk. Starting off he was clowned on for wanting to start an electric car company, now he is revered as one of the greatest innovators the world ever knew. Your goals may be unrealistic and strange, but everything great that ever came about started off as an unrealistic and strange idea. Be creative, be unrealistic and take action now!

This book is part of LIONS DEN productions. It is intended to help you improve every aspect of your life, although we aren't held liable for the improvement of your life. This is information produced to help you take the first step. With everything ACTION is required, lack of results are not the responsibility of the authors of this book. We wish you success, happiness and a fulfilling life. Please feel free to check out our other material that may also help you get on the right track of your personal endeavors.

LIONS DEN PODCAST

https://anchor.fm/julio-andrino

https://podcasts.apple.com/us/podcast/lions-den/id1475256408

In this podcast we talk about Leadership and Mindset development. Being a strong LEADER and having an elevated MINDSET are the top traits that separate the average and ordinary from the successful and extraordinary.